Is my dog a genius?

Is my dog a genius?

This edition published in 2022

By SJG Gift Publishing, HP22 6NF, UK

Author: Helen Redding

Images used under license from Shutterstock.com

Cover design: Milestone Creative

Contents design: Jo Ross, Double Fish Design Ltd

ISBN: 978-1-913004-99-6

Printed in China

10 9 8 7 6 5 4 3 2 1

If you think dogs can't count, try putting three dog biscuits in your pocket and then give him only two of them.

PHIL PASTORET

Contents

Introduction 7

Brainy basics

How clever are dogs? 10

What is intelligence? 14

Dogs' brains: ten top facts 16

Signs of super intelligence 19

Different breeds, different brains 22

Testing and feeding the brain

Spotting a clever puppy 28

Doggy IQ tests 32

Healthy dog, clever dog 37

Brain games: math for mutts 40

Canine senses

Doggy senses 44

Sixth sense – fact or fiction? 47

Working together

Can you create a genius? 52

Communication skills 56

Brain games: chores 60

Social skills 63

Famous geniuses and their dogs 68

Memory

Marvellous memories 74

Now you see it … 78

Brain games: the classics 80

Unlock your dog's potential

Keeping your dog stimulated 86

Canine wordsmiths 91

Tricky tricks 95

Every dog is unique

Clever dogs: the downsides 102

Brain games: walkies! 106

Less intelligent dogs: the upsides! 109

Older dogs 113

The lighter side of genius

Top dog geniuses 118

Just for fun 122

Test your knowledge! 126

Genius training notes 128

No one appreciates the very special genius of your conversation as much as the dog does.

CHRISTOPHER MORLEY

Introduction

We all adore our dogs. They're sometimes smelly and frequently get under our feet, but we love them. They each have their own wonderful personalities and quirks. Perhaps they're the funniest dog or the most caring dog. You may even think they're the cleverest dog in the world. But are they really or are you simply blinded by love?

So, how do you know if your dog is a genius? In this book, you'll discover how dogs' brains work and gain an invaluable insight into their behavior. Find out what 'normal' doggy behavior is and what might indicate that your pooch has superior intelligence. You can even try an IQ test.

Remember, if your dog doesn't turn out to be the Einstein of the canine world, they're still the most wonderfully slobbery creature and you wouldn't swap them for the world. Or your dog might be gifted with one type of genius but not with another – let's celebrate them all!

Dogs like to obey.
It gives them security.

JAMES HERRIOT

Brainy
basics

How clever are dogs?

It's fair to say that we consider some dogs to be cleverer than others: think the military sniffer dog versus the pet dog that crazily chases its own tail and is surprised by its own farts. Most of the research into canine intelligence suggests that dogs function at the same level as an average two-year-old child. Given that most people say that having a dog is like having a child, this won't be a surprise! Dogs aren't simply about where the next bowl of food comes from or where the stick lands; their brains are actually pretty impressive.

Social cognition

Social cognition refers to the role that brain processes play in social interaction. Dogs are fairly advanced in this because they're social animals and need to be good at understanding subtle social signals and gestures from members of their social group (other dogs or humans). A good example of this is pointing. If you point at something, chances are your dog will look at where you're pointing rather than at your hand. They may do the same with even subtler gestures such as following your gaze.

Love and bonding

When dogs seem pleased to see you, they genuinely are! As far as they're concerned, we're part of their family and they love us. When you make eye contact with your dog, oxytocin – the 'love hormone' – is released in their body. Yes, they love you THAT much and it's an important part of bonding with them.

Dogs are very sensitive to our emotions and can adjust their behavior accordingly. Think about a time when you felt sad – how has your dog behaved? It's likely that they'll have given you more attention, perhaps cuddling up next to you. This is a sign of their capacity for empathy – the ability to understand and share the feelings of others. They respond to emotive sounds, such as laughter and crying, just as humans do.

But...

It's not all good news for our canine friends! Research conducted in 2018 suggests that, compared to other animals, dogs aren't quite as smart as we like to think. The research compared dogs to other domesticated animals such as cats, pigs, goats, pigeons and horses. What did the results show?

- Sensory cognition: smell, hearing, taste, and touch – dogs were no more advanced than the other animals.

- Physical cognition: interacting with the environment, for example, treat puzzles – dogs can learn to repeat tasks, but they aren't so good at working out solutions for themselves.

- Spatial cognition: on-the-ground geography and navigation – dogs are very good at remembering places but aren't good at simple navigational tasks, such as figuring out how to walk around a wall to get to an owner calling them from the other side. Pigeons manage this far better!

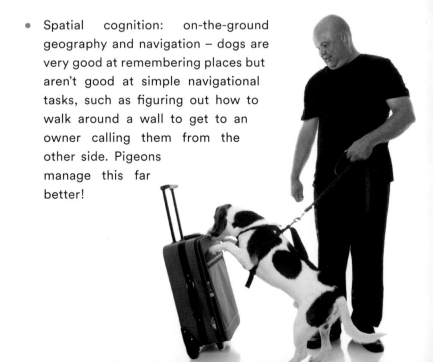

PAWS FOR THOUGHT

Did you know that, like a two-year-old child, the cleverest dogs can learn up to 250 words and gestures? Even with just basic training, most dogs can learn around 165 words. They can also count to five!

- Social cognition: dogs did well in this area compared to other creatures (such as cats that don't seem to care what anyone else does!). However, goats, pigs and dolphins are at least as good as dogs at following human pointing.

- Self-consciousness: does a dog know that it is a dog? Nope. Dogs are unable to recognize themselves in a mirror – apparently even ants can do that! – and that's a sign of a serious lack of smartness.

Overall, the research concluded that dogs share a cleverness level with cats, pigs and goats, but limp along behind chimpanzees and dolphins. In some ways, dogs aren't even as smart as pigeons. Fortunately, we do know that they're brilliant at being dogs!!

What is intelligence?

As you'll discover throughout the book, there's no single definition of what makes an intelligent dog. The same applies to humans! Someone who is amazing at art but terrible at math is no less intelligent that someone else who excels at math but can't draw to save their lives. So, what are the different types of intelligence that dogs have?

The three types of canine cleverness

According to the renowned researcher, psychologist and author of numerous dog books, Professor Stanley Coren, dog intelligence can be split into three types:

Instinct intelligence

This is mainly down to your dog's breed. Basically, retrievers are good at retrieving things, sheepdogs are good at herding sheep, guard dogs are good are watching over things… and so on and so on. Your dog will inherit this intelligence as part of its make-up.

Adaptive intelligence

This is what your dog can learn to do for itself. It's your dog's ability to learn quickly from observing you and the environment and from its experiences. Problem solving, logic and reasoning are all part of this.

Working and obedience intelligence

This is what your dog can learn by being trained and instructed by you. It's their ability to listen, understand and respond to you. Working and obedience intelligence is what you think of most when considering whether your dog is a genius.

PAWS FOR THOUGHT

A canine IQ test isn't an accurate measure of your dog's intelligence if you're looking at them as a whole and factoring in the three types of intelligence. The tests are helpful though, in measuring problem solving and memory skills. See Doggy IQ tests on page 32.

Dogs' brains:
ten top facts

Dogs are amazing creatures. If you've ever wondered what makes your dog's brain tick, here are some fascinating facts. You might start to look at your dog in a different light. Unfortunately, unless dogs start talking to us, there's a lot that we'll never know.

1. A dog's brain is considerably smaller than a human brain compared to overall body size. A human brain weighs in at 1/50th of our body weight. Compare that to the 1/125th ratio for a dog!

2. The part of a dog's brain that processes smell is 40 times bigger than it is in a human brain. Coupled with the 250 million smell receptors in their nose (compare that to our 5 million), you'll understand why dogs have such an impressive sense of smell!

3. When they sleep, dogs have very similar brain activity to humans. When they twitch in their sleep they're dreaming. Research suggests they're probably dreaming about familiar activities like chasing their tail or playing outside. And no, we've no idea either how scientists discovered this! Interestingly, small dogs dream more than big dogs.

4. Research has shown that dogs, like humans, are capable of feeling emotions such as optimism, anxiety, happiness, fear, jealousy and depression. There is also evidence that dogs that experience traumatic events can can suffer from symptoms of PTSD, just like humans do.

5. The structure of a dog's brain is very similar to that of a human brain. An important part of a dog's brain is the striatum. It's rich in dopamine and manages reward, pleasure and expectation – probably the three most important things in a dog's world!

6. About one-third of dogs are right-pawed, one third left-pawed and the rest have no preference. Right-pawed dogs are more likely to pass the Assistance Dog training as they tend to be bolder and more inquisitive. Left-pawed dogs tend to be more aggressive.

7. Dogs go through their developmental stages much more quickly than humans do. By the time they're 4–6 months old, they've attained their full emotional range.

8. Dogs can have either an optimistic or a pessimistic personality. A study showed that some dogs were always keen to investigate a place where there was a 50:50 chance of food, but others were reluctant to take the risk. So, it seems that just like with humans, some dogs hope for the best, whilst others expect the worst!

9. Thinking about their owner makes a dog feel happy! Brain scans revealed that when scientists present dogs with the smell of their owner, it activates the part of their brain connected to rewards and gives them a feeling of security. Awww.

10. Dogs learn through association – that is, the consequences of their actions. If their behavior has a positive outcome, they're likely to repeat it. Hopefully, the same works in reverse! That's why it's so important to be consistent when training your dog: if they get the same positive result when they repeat an action, it is more likely to become embedded in their brains.

Signs of
super intelligence

So, you think you've got a clever dog on your hands? A really clever dog? We always think our dog is the brightest and best and there's very little that will dissuade us from this. Telling everyone you meet about your dog's abilities demonstrates pride and love all rolled into one. But how can you tell if they really are more intelligent than the average dog on the street? What should you look out for?

Sign #1 – Long term memory

Did you once teach your dog an amazing trick or command but then the novelty wore off and it became a distant memory? Well, if your dog can still remember it after a long break it's a sign that they're super smart. Just as with humans though, your dog's memory can deteriorate with age so do bear that in mind.

Sign #2 – Escape artists

Let your dog out of one door, close it and open a different door. If your dog can find its way back in through the open door when the door it originally exited through is closed, it's a sign of high intelligence. It shows your dog is thinking outside the box and finding a solution to a problem.

Sign #3 – Holiday blues

Does your dog behave strangely when you get your suitcase out? They might get in it or even try to hide it, and perhaps they become very clingy. If your dog is intelligent, it is adept at observing your behavior and can anticipate what's coming – in this instance that you might be leaving them to go on holiday. Your dog will make similar observations of its surroundings (and draw catastrophic conclusions) when there's an impending vet's trip!

Sign #4 – Letting you take the lead (not that lead!)

A clever dog knows to look to its owner for instruction and guidance. Your dog might be awesome at following your orders, but if it also anticipates a change in situation and physically looks to you for cues as to what to do, that's the sign of an extra special pooch.

Sign #5 – Avoiding risk

A dog that is averse to risk has a higher level of intelligence. Next time you cross a road, observe whether your dog stops at the curb without being asked to. If they do, they're cleverly assessing risk and acting accordingly. You may notice that they do the same in any situation where they don't feel entirely safe, for example when meeting a new person.

Sign #6 – Empathy

A super smart dog can understand your feelings and will try to make you feel better. Awww. When you're feeling sad or have had a terrible day at work, it will come and cuddle you or stick closely by your side. If your dog tunes in with your feelings then they're not only intelligent, they're a keeper!

Different breeds,
different brains

Before you leave a copy of *War and Peace* in your dog's basket, research has found that some breeds of dog are cleverer than others. To be blunt, your dog might be better off with a copy of *The Very Hungry Caterpillar*. But don't count your dog out if it's not top of the list of brainy breeds – every dog is an individual and, whilst their behavior is dictated somewhat by their breed, their personality still shines through.

Why are some dogs cleverer than others?

It's all in their heritage and breeding. Dogs bred to follow commands, such as Collies and Retrievers, are more intelligent that those dogs bred to hunt or to be powerful. Bulldogs, for example, have been bred for strength; they didn't need to be clever to perform for the jobs they did and this has carried down to the breed as it is today. If a dog is easily trained, they tend to be more intelligent – that's why you see Labrador Retrievers and German Shepherds used as law enforcement dogs.

Top 10 brainy breeds

1. Border Collie

2. Poodle

3. German Shepherd

4. Golden Retriever

5. Doberman Pinscher

6. Shetland sheepdog

7. Labrador Retriever

8. Papillon

9. Bloodhound

10. Rottweiler

Why are Border Collies so clever?

Collies were bred to be working dogs, which is key to their brain power. They learn fast and are quick to follow commands, making them perfect for tasks like herding sheep. Collies are highly motivated and absolutely love having a job to do. This isn't to say there aren't some very daft Collie dogs out there!

And bottom of the class?

Not all dogs are as easy to train, adaptable or intelligent as those breeds listed on the previous page. But that doesn't mean they're not loving, fun or a pleasure to have at your side. It's all about what you want in a pet and each breed has its own positives. If you don't own a flock of sheep, will you really get to see your Border Collie's super brain at work?!

Some of the least intelligent – but equally lovely – breeds include: Basset Hounds, Beagles, Mastiffs and Bulldogs. The beautiful Afghan Hound is considered the least intelligent breed because of its extremely low obedience level and unwillingness to respond to commands. That said, what they might lack in brains they certainly make up for in personality, looks and flowing locks!

Everyone thinks they have the best dog. And none of them are wrong.

W. R. PURCHE

Everything I know
I learned from dogs.

NORA ROBERTS

Testing and feeding the brain

Spotting a
clever puppy

It's not easy to tell at a very early stage if you've got a doggy genius on your hands. Puppies' brains are not fully developed until they're around four weeks old. Their sense of sight doesn't fully develop until 7–8 weeks. And just like humans, it takes a while for their full sense of coordination to become established (and for them to lose their kooky cuteness!).

Early days

The ability to learn quickly and follow commands is a good sign of a clever dog... but don't expect this of puppies. Whilst you can get a clear sense of their personality and how alert they are, their cognitive functions aren't fully developed so you're unlikely to be able to judge how clever they'll eventually be. Any time before eight weeks is too early to be putting their name down for an Ivy League college!

The intelligence that your puppy grows up with depends on a combination of factors: how they're handled, their early experiences, socialization and, of course, their breed. No two puppies are alike and within a litter you'll see a wide range of differences in personalities and learning ability.

Help them bloom

You can't measure a puppy's brain power when they're very young, but you can help them to bloom by giving them lots of mental stimulation. Play with them and provide them with toys to keep their brains ticking and help their neural pathways make links. You can't create intelligence, but you can help it along. However, you'll notice that at an early age they're VERY clever at doing the things they need to survive – i.e. finding their mother's milk and a warm space to sleep! The rest will follow, particularly as their brain and physical abilities start to synchronize.

Puppy IQ test

If you look online, there are a whole range of IQ tests available for dogs and puppies (in fact, probably for any animal if you search hard enough!). They're fun to do but that's the key word: FUN. Every puppy is adorable whatever score they get so don't take these tests too seriously. If anything, use them to bond with your pup and enjoy some quality time together.

Here are some quick tests to try:

● Observation test

Choose an activity that you and your puppy have done many times before, for example, going for a walk. When you step towards the door or pick up the lead, what does your puppy do? If they immediately understand that you're intending to go for a walk, then they have excellent observation skills.

PAWS FOR THOUGHT

Don't try an IQ test before your dog is 12 weeks old. They should also have been living with you for over four weeks.

● Problem solving

All you need for this is an empty can or cup and one of your pup's favorite treats. Show your puppy the treat and then put it under the upturned can. If they get to the treat by knocking over the can in under 15 seconds, they're a top dog! The longer they take, the less developed their problem-solving skills.

● Social learning

Look directly into your puppy's eyes and smile. If they come towards you immediately, this is awesome and shows they have good social learning.

● Short term memory

Show your puppy a treat and then let them see you place it under a blanket. Pick up your puppy, walk them around the room and then place them down at least six feet away from the blanket. If they're super clever, they'll remember where the treat is and go straight to it. If they show no interest, it's likely that their short term memory is currently pretty bad!

Doggy
IQ tests

Everyone loves testing how good they are at something. Whether it's a magazine quiz about how good a friend we are or a carnival strength test, being able to rate ourselves is endlessly fascinating. There's really no reason to test your dog's IQ. So why do we do it? Possibly to impress other dog owners on the daily walk or just for bragging rights. The most important thing is: don't take IQ tests too seriously!

● Are IQ tests useful?

IQ tests only provide a narrow definition of intelligence. With humans, IQ tests focus on reading, writing, logic and analytical thinking – these are all a good measure of whether a person will excel academically. However, what about all those people who didn't do well at school, but we still call a 'genius'? For example, the entrepreneurs who came up with hugely successful ideas but never went to college.

A 'genius' in one area might not be a genius in another. It's all relative. IQ tests will measure certain areas of your dog's cognitive abilities, but they won't capture how brilliant your dog is at, for example, reading your emotions and knowing when to give you a cuddle.

The standard tests

Search on the internet and you'll find a plethora of canine intelligence tests. The standard (and probably most reliable) tests were developed by well-known neuropsychologist and dog expert, Professor Stanley Coren.

Try some of the following tests, based on Professor Coren's work.

TEST 1 – PROBLEM SOLVING

Place a large towel or blanket over your dog's head.

SCORES: Three points if your dog works out how to free itself in less than 15 seconds. Two points if it takes 15 to 30 seconds. One point if it takes more than 30 seconds.

TEST 2 – MORE PROBLEM SOLVING

Put one of your dog's favorite treats on the floor and cover it with a towel. Time how long it takes your dog to find it.

SCORES: Three points if your dog finds it in under 15 seconds. Two points if it takes 15 to 60 seconds. One point for more than 60 seconds.

TEST 3 – INFORMATION RETENTION

Put two or three cups upside down in front of your dog. Hide a treat under one of the containers (with your dog watching). Try and distract them for a few seconds and then let them seek out the treat.

SCORES: Three points if they get the cup hiding the treat right first time. Two points if they get it right second time. One point if they choose two wrong cups before finding the right one.

TEST 4 – REASONING

Place a treat underneath a piece of furniture that's low enough for only your dog's paw to fit under.

SCORES: Three points if your dog takes less than 60 seconds to reach it successfully. Two points if it tries to reach the food with its head rather than its paw. One point if your dog can't be bothered to try and gives up entirely!

TEST 5 – MORE REASONING AND PROBLEM SOLVING!

Make a barrier using cardboard or furniture that's too tight for your dog to squeeze through and too high for them to jump over. Through a gap, show them a treat and encourage them to get it (do this for around a minute).

SCORE: Three points if your dog takes less than 30 seconds to work out that they need to walk around the barrier you've made to reach the treat. Two points for more than 30 seconds. One point if your impatient pooch tries to squeeze through the gap instead of going around the obstacle!

How did they do?

- 13–15 points: Your dog is a genius – well, at these tasks anyway!

- 9–12 points: Pretty smart pooch.

- 5–8 points: Your dog wasn't first in line when brains were given out but with a little work they could do better.

- 1–4 points: Eek. Your dog probably won't be heading off to college so focus on all their other positives.

Help – my dog is useless!

So, your dog doesn't perform well in IQ tests. What should you do? Should you give up? No! There are things you can do to unlock their potential. It might not be a huge potential, but you can give them a chance to do their best!

- If you're using treats, make sure they're ones your dog finds delicious. If they're not bothered about the reward, they won't work for it.

- Puzzles and interactive toys can enhance and stimulate your dog's brain.

- As always, be patient! Your hard work will pay off but whether that's 'now' or 'eventually' will very much depend on your dog.

See also Can You Create a Genius? (page 52) for more tips on how to boost your dog's brain.

Healthy dog
clever dog

Humans are becoming more and more aware of the link between physical health and mental health. Looking after your mind is just as important as looking after your body – in fact, you cannot separate the two. The same applies to dogs. An unhealthy dog will not be a happy dog and is unlikely to be able to function as well as it should.

Brain food for dogs

In the 1950s and 60s, people in the UK were told to 'go to work on an egg'. This was seen as the perfect start to the day. More recently, a whole industry has grown around brain foods and superfoods. Green smoothies, acai berries and kale are all the rage for humans – but what should you be feeding your doggy genius to keep their brain in tiptop condition? Much like us, dogs can benefit from superfoods, too.

Feeding your dog foods that are rich in vitamins, fatty acids and antioxidants has been shown to improve intelligence and cognitive abilities. Get their diet right and you can maximize their intelligence and help them get better at following commands and responding to you – no more embarrassing displays of your lack of authority in the park!

Getting your dog's diet right

A healthy dog needs to have a balanced diet that includes a good variety of foods providing a range of proteins, fats, vitamins and minerals. For starters, choose a dog food that's made with high quality and easily digestible ingredients – with the minimum of artificial additives.

Ditch the unhealthy, processed treats and swap in nutrient-rich nibbles such as cooked sweet potatoes, pumpkin and carrots. (Holistic health practitioners also believe that vegetables can provide a stabilizing energy that focuses the mind.)

Docosahexaenoic acid, or DHA, is a type of Omega-3 fat and

is proven to improve brain function and mental development. Foods rich in DHA – such as salmon and salmon oil – can improve learning abilities and short-term memory. (This is especially helpful at the puppy stage and during the first year of their life when they're growing at their fastest.)

Here are five of the top superfoods to boost brainpower:

1. Salmon and salmon oil – rich in Omega-3's DHA and EPA

2. Rosemary extract – vitamin D, antioxidants

3. Peas – vitamins C and E, antioxidants

4. Sweet potato – beta carotene and chlorogenic acid

5. Maize – antioxidants lutein and zeaxanthin.

PAWS FOR THOUGHT

When a puppy is 10 days old, it only has a few hundred neural connections per brain cell. Fast forward to 35 days old and the number of connections for each neuron multiplies to around 12,000!

Brain games:
math for mutts

Games involving numbers will be a huge challenge for your dog's brain. They may reveal themselves as a mathematical genius or they may stare at you blankly – it's not so different with humans! As counting is one of the trickiest activities to do with a dog, you'll need lots of patience and a pocketful (or three or four) of treats.

One, two, three

Aim of the game: Teach your dog to 'count' using barks. Okay, so they're not really counting but no one else knows that! It will definitely get your dog thinking, though. (It's helpful for this activity if your dog can bark on command.)

Step 1:

With your dog sitting in front of you, make eye contact and hold a treat in your hand.

Step 2:

Raise your hand (the one without the treat in it) and prompt your dog to bark. Drop your hand. One bark gets the treat.

Step 3:

Repeat the above but wait until your dog barks twice. After the second bark, drop your hand and look away (this is the important bit!), then reward your dog with the treat.

Step 4:

Keep repeating the above with an extra bark each time. Eventually, your dog will learn to keep barking until you lower your hand and look away. Then you can start doing math to impress people! Ask your dog what two add two is then hold up your hand until they've barked four times. They're a genius!

If dogs could talk, perhaps we would find it as hard to get along with them as we do with people.

CAPEK

Canine senses

Doggy
senses

The structure of a dog's brain is very similar to that of humans and other mammals. Thankfully, humans are much more advanced at processing information and thoughts because of our highly developed prefrontal cortex – which is the reason we keep dogs and not vice versa! However, we're certainly not top dog in all areas. Canine senses are quite incredible compared to ours and understanding how they work gives us an amazing insight into how dogs' brains function.

Sight

- Great low-light vision. Dogs have much bigger pupils and a higher ratio of rods to cones than humans – this means that they only need around one fifth of the light that we need to see. Which is handy because dogs can't hold flashlights.

- Awesome peripheral vision – but only if, like a dog, your eyes are on the side of your head. With our very boring front-facing eyes, humans only have 180 degrees of peripheral vision (how we'd love eyes in the back of our head!). Dogs, however, can have up to 250 degrees of vision.

Hearing

- High frequency hearing. Dogs can hear frequencies up to 45 kHz. This means they have fantastic hearing (compare humans: we only hear up to 20 kHz), but it's not all good news. A sound with a frequency higher than 36 kHz can be painful for dogs and prompt whining and barking.

- Magnificent muscles. Dogs have over 18 muscles in their ears that allow them to be tilted, rotated, lowered and raised, and do everything bar the Hokey Pokey. This allows them to focus on and locate sounds precisely – one of the skills that makes dogs ideal for rescue operations.

- Multi-tasking ears. Now this is something! Each ear can hear independently, which means that dogs can listen to two different sounds at once.

Taste

Okay so here's something we do beat dogs at! The human tongue has 9,000 taste buds compared to dogs' tongues which have just 1,700. However, it's well known that taste and smell are connected – just think how you lose your sense of taste when your nose is blocked with a cold – so with their super noses dogs probably have still got us beat!

Smell

- AKA, your dog's Super Sense that they use to gather information from the world around them. A dog has an incredible 250 MILLION smell receptors in their nose! Humans have a pretty lame five million – quite pathetic in comparison.

- The part of their brain that a dog uses to process smells is 40 times bigger than the same part in a human brain.

- Dogs move the nostrils independently to determine the direction a smell is coming from. Us mere mortals must move our whole heads.

PAWS FOR THOUGHT

Most people believe that dogs can only see in black and white. In fact, they only see in shades of yellow and blue.

Sixth sense –
fact or fiction?

If there's one thing that might lead you to believe your dog is a genius, it's their uncanny ability to detect things before they happen. Whether it's getting excited before the doorbell has even rung or sensing a monumental earthquake is on the way, dogs seem to have a mysterious sixth sense. But is pretty lame five magical or something more mundane?

Dogs can predict earthquakes

FACT! But it's not down to mystical powers of divination. Dogs can tune in to very high frequency sound, which means they can hear and detect the subtle shifting in the ground even before an earthquake happens. They become agitated and that's their warning sign.

Dogs are weather vanes

FACT! Dogs start to act strangely if there's a storm on the way. Humans can 'smell rain in the air' but dogs' magnificent noses can pick up that change in the atmosphere long before we do. They're also far more sensitive to barometric pressure than we are so they can sense the drop in pressure that an approaching storm brings. Plus, it's likely that dogs can feel the vibrations of distant thunder through their paws.

Dogs can detect illness

FACT! We know that dogs have incredible noses and we're discovering more and more about their olfactory ability. 'Seizure alert and response' trained dogs can tell if a person is about to have an epileptic seizure and so warn them. By detecting a change in the smell of someone's breath, dogs can also warn diabetics if their blood sugar is dropping to potentially dangerous levels. Amazingly, it's possible that dogs can also detect the presence of cancer and if someone is about to go into labor.

Dogs know when you're on your way home

FACT! But how?! They can't tell the time. They can't hear you if you're still some distance away. Your dog isn't psychic, but what they do have is a sense of time passing. They love familiarity and quickly become accustomed to your daily routine (especially if you're boringly predictable!). Whilst they may not know for sure that you're on your way, they make a very good guess based on their internal clock and their (high) expectations of you!

When it comes to 'predicting' the future, yes, your dog certainly is a genius – well, more so than humans anyway. But it isn't anything magical and you certainly won't be letting your dog run a 'Psychic Night' at the local town hall; their ability is all down to the amazing range of their senses.

PAWS FOR THOUGHT

Can dogs sense paranormal activity? If your dog has ever stared intently at a particular spot or barked at something that isn't there, you may have found it a little spooky. No one knows if dogs can see things that we can't – all we know is there's a lot in this world we still don't know about!

There is only one smartest dog in the world, and every boy has it.

ANON

Working together

Can you create
a genius?

You already know that thanks to breeding, some types of dog are naturally cleverer than others. That's not to say that every dog that belongs to a 'clever' breed is a genius – there are always exceptions! But how much of a dog's brain power comes from what they're born with and how much is from what they learn from other dogs and from us? Is there anything we can do to boost their brain?

Understanding how dogs learn

We all learn things in different ways and knowing how we learn can help us. For example, some people have a photographic memory that allows them to store whole pages of a book in their head, whilst others can only remember a shopping list by turning it into a song! If you can understand how your dog learns, you can help them make the most of their brain. Keep in mind that every interaction you have with your dog is training – they're constantly learning.

Association

Association is the key method by which a dog learns new skills and how to behave. This applies from their very early days and throughout their lives. They're quite simple beings, really. If an action or behavior has a positive outcome, your dog will repeat it, hoping for the same result. For example, if your dog learns that sitting when asked to earns it a treat, it will very happily carry on doing it so long as the treats keep coming! The same principle applies if if your dog misbehaves: denying it an expected treat should help prevent bad habits from forming!

Reaching their potential

It's all well and good knowing that your dog learns by association but how do you help that happen? (Otherwise you might never tap into your dog's genius!)

- Be consistent: Repeating the same command over and over again is the most effective way to fix an expected response in your dog's mind. But because they learn by association, you must be CONSISTENT. It's no good repeating something if the training outcome or your reaction is different every time – your dog won't know if they're getting it right or wrong!

- Counter-conditioning: Negative experiences early in a dog's life can affect their behavior going forward. For example, a bad experience with another dog might make them nervous of all unfamiliar dogs. The good news is that these experiences needn't hold them back: with time and patience you can replace a negative association with a positive one.

- Effective communication: You'll get the best from your dog if you can communicate clearly with them. There should be no doubt over what you're trying to say. The most important lesson is, of course, the difference between 'yes' and 'no'. Teaching them through association is the best way to achieve this. If your dog understands 'yes' means 'go ahead' or 'good' and 'no' means 'stop' or 'bad' then there's nothing you can't teach them!

Brain training

Brain training is a way of exercising the mind and improving cognitive skills. Whole books have been written about brain training dogs, but we have one perfectly formed chapter to help you have fun with your canine genius – see page 95. You'll also find a selection of brain games dotted throughout the book.

PAWS FOR THOUGHT

With any doggy behavior,
if a wild dog doesn't do it, it isn't
natural behavior and is
therefore learned.

Communication
skills

Good communication between you and your dog is vital for a happy pet – and a happy owner! As we discovered in the last section, working together will encourage your dog to fulfil its potential. They cannot learn from you unless they understand what you're trying to communicate, so be super-clear and give them the best chance of showing you just how clever they are. Your dog may be a genius, but you'll never know if you don't help them show you!

Signs of confusion

Let's be frank: if your dog is confused, it's because you've failed to provide clear instructions. Look out for these signs that your dog needs YOU to do better!

- Lies down on the floor and completely ignores you.

- Gets overexcited and is easily startled.

- Ignores the treats they normally love.

- Barks at other dogs.

When you spot that your dog is confused about what you expect from them, it's time to take a break. Their canine brain can't understand what you want from them. If you want your dog to be a genius, don't push them too hard – and definitely don't get frustrated with them. Just relax (both of you!) and take a moment before you return to what you were doing.

If you're trying to teach your dog something – perhaps a trick or a new command – the general rule is that if they don't understand it within two attempts, you've set the difficulty level too high. Take the level down a notch and work your way back up gradually. Even the brightest of dogs won't pick up a new command or skill immediately.

Build a bond

Once dogs and their owners have built a bond, it's almost impossible to break. To do this, good communication is vital, as it helps your dog develop trust in you. As always, consistency is key: if they know that following your commands will bring the same responses each time, your dog will trust you. And with that trust comes a feeling of security that's crucial for getting the best out of your four-legged friend. Pay them lots of attention by petting, grooming and playing together and you'll have a friend for life.

PAWS FOR THOUGHT

When a dog looks at your face, they are taking in your emotions. According to research, dogs are the only animals that can see at a glance if we are happy, sad or angry.

Make it two-way

To build a strong bond with your dog, communication must go both ways. Don't get so absorbed in what you're saying that you forget to listen to and observe your dog. Their messages can be very subtle so have quiet moments where you're simply aware of your dog and what they're trying to communicate to you. Don't assume you always know what your dog is trying to tell you. For example, when your dog brings you a favorite toy, they're not always asking to play – they're offering you their possession to mark your role as leader.

The stronger the bond you build with your dog, the more their intelligence and ability to learn new things will develop.

Brain games:
chores

We all have busy lives, which can make it difficult for us to give our pets as much attention as we – and they! – might like. time is tight, why not incorporate some doggy brain work into your everyday routine?
(Secret: these activities will help you around the house too!)

Tidy up

Aim of the game: Teach your dog to become a canine garbage collector.

Step 1: Place an item of garbage, for example, or some an old newspaper on the floor. Encourage your dog to fetch the item and bring it to you. With your trash can at the ready, instruct

them to 'drop' it inside. Reward them with lots of praise and a treat.

Step 2: Practice, repeat, practice, repeat! Try different items and try putting them in different spots around the room, some close to the trash can, some far away.

Step 3: As your dog gets used to the activity, start to move yourself further away from the trash can. You'll then break any association between your presence and the action.

Step 4: All being well – and no doubt with considerable practice! – you'll end up being able to simply point out an item on the floor and your clever pooch will know to put it in the garbage. (Warning: if anything goes missing, check the trash can! You might have an overenthusiastic dog.)

This activity is a great way to get your dog to focus on following instructions, finding items and completing a task. They'll also love doing a job and being praised for it. Dogs are easily pleased. For them it's fun, for you, it's one less job to do!

You can also expand their learning and apply it to other items around the house. Teach your dog to retrieve your keys to save you hunting around for them every time you leave home. Why not teach your dog everyone's name and how to 'find' them in the morning. Getting the family out of bed has never been easier!

Social
skills

Every dog has its own personality but knowing what to expect from your dog's social behavior will help you understand if their interpersonal skills are normal or extraordinary. Of course, if your dog greets a visitor by sitting on their hind legs and holding out a paw to shake hands, you can be certain your courteous canine is a genius!

The basics

Like some humans, many dogs lack basic social skills. And, as with humans, these should really be taught at an early age. However, as an adult dog has the same level of social awareness as a two-year-old you shouldn't expect TOO much of them. Turn the page to find out what your dog should be capable of doing by the time they are out of puppyhood...

- Play well with other dogs.

- Interact calmly with humans of all ages and not jump up at visitors.

- React calmly to noisy stimuli in the home and outside – for example, vacuums, children's toys, car, bicycles.

- Be able to fit in with your activities – for example, a visit to a café.

(N.B. Not all geniuses of the human variety are blessed with good social skills so it's unfair to assume your dog will have been! However, if your dog has been taught appropriate social behavior – and practises it consistently – that's a pretty good sign of a clever brain at work.)

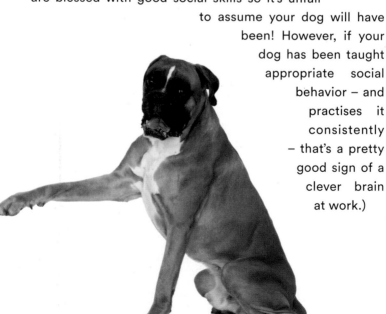

Safe and secure

The best way to teach your dog social skills is by helping them learn that the world isn't a scary place. This involves exposing them to different situations, environments and people, and ensuring they feel secure in all of them.

To help your dog feel safe, you should always work at a level where they feel completely comfortable. Watch their body language and be alert to signs they're starting to feel stressed. If they become uncomfortable, lower the intensity of whatever is triggering their discomfort or leave that environment. As they grow accustomed to new situations, gradually build up your dog's confidence by introducing more people, longer distances, louder noises, etc.

Reward your dog with a treat when they have obeyed your commands and remember to tell them what a good job they've done!

Playing nicely

If you want your dog to be the envy of other owners you need to teach them how to play nicely with other dogs. This dogs will stimulate your dog's mind and keep them feeling happy, but not always easy to tell the difference between good play and play that's got out of hand. Growling and biting can be part of normal fun, but look out for the body language that says your dog (or their companion) is playing too rough:

- When bouncing around changes to quick, darting movements.

- Lips curled.

- Ears pinned back.

- Stiff body.

The best way to teach your dog appropriate play is to socialize them with other dogs from an early age. At the puppy stage, if something hurts, they'll yelp and let their playmate know. Without this trial and error, it's hard for dogs to learn how to interact. But that doesn't mean you can't teach an old dog new tricks:

- Obedience is vital. If you know your dog will rapidly obey your commands, you'll be able to...

- ...stop a tricky situation developing. Watch your dog while it's playing and if they display any of the signs from page 66, call an end to the fun and games.

- Conditioning: you can use treats (of course!) to make your dog feel comfortable and calm. As soon as they encounter other dogs and start to show signs of nervousness, give them some treats so that they have a positive rather than a negative association with the situation. The calmer they are with other dogs, the more likely they are to play nicely.

Your dog will gradually come to understand that overexcited behavior that borders on aggression will end in a Time Out... and a clever dog will realize that that's no fun at all.

Famous geniuses
and their
dogs

Let's turn the tables and see which geniuses from history were dog lovers. Of course, their pets were clearly hugely influential and they wouldn't have been half as clever without them. So, which came first: the genius or their dog?!

Albert Einstein

This genius of theoretical physics was a well-known pet lover. When talking about his dog, Chico Marx, a Fox Terrier, he said: "The dog is very smart. He feels sorry for me because I receive so much mail. That's why he tries to bite the mailman." Apparently, Einstein was hugely inspired by his pet cats, too – but let's not talk about that here!

Andy Warhol

In the 1970s, Pop Art legend, Andy Warhol, acquired a Dachshund named Archie. Warhol and Archie were inseparable and the dog often accompanied his owner to interviews. Warhol would deflect any questions to his dog if he didn't want to answer them. That's genius and eccentricity for you!

Pablo Picasso

Picasso is another artist in a long list of creative geniuses who loved dogs and animals of all kinds. His most famous canine companion was a Dachshund called Lump, who accompanied him everywhere. Lump was immortalized in many of Picasso's works and their relationship even inspired a book written by Lump's original owner.

Lord Bryon

This famed poet and aristocrat had a beloved pet called Boatswain, a black and white Newfoundland. When Boatswain died of rabies, Bryon memorialized him in marble. On his tomb (which is larger than his owner's) is Byron's poem, 'Epitaph to a Dog'. At one point Byron owned ten horses, eight dogs, three monkeys, five cats, an eagle, a crow, a falcon, five peacocks, two guinea hens and an Egyptian crane!

Alfred Hitchcock

Hitchcock was an incredible filmmaker whose movies sent chills down our spines – but he had a softer side which was demonstrated by his love of dogs. Hitchcock was infatuated with Sealyham Terriers, a breed which are notoriously difficult to train. However, Hitchcock seemed to do a great job of it, with two of his beloved dogs making a cameo appearance alongside him in his 1963 film, *The Birds*.

Intelligent dogs rarely want to please people whom they do not respect.

W. R. KOEHLER

A dog is nothing but a furry person.

ANON

Memory

Marvellous
memories

No, we're not talking about the time your dog destroyed your new couch or when they 'helped' your neighbor dig up their garden. Here, we're interested in how good your dog's short- and long-term memory is, and whether it's an indicator of their intelligence. The more we learn about dogs' brains the more we understand how similar they are to the human brain.

The basics

Memory is vital for wild or domestic dogs. It has an important part to play in how they navigate their environment, hunt prey, find food, recognize people and learn new skills. Your dog's strongest sense is its sense of smell, so whilst they do use visual memories, they tend to rely heavily on the scent of things. Research suggests that dogs can remember smells for years.

Plus, they can link smell to their emotional memory – just like humans do.

A dog's short-term memory lasts for about five minutes – longer than a goldfish, not as long as their arch rivals, cats. Their long-term memory is much harder to determine. It's clear that dogs do have a reasonably good long-term memory as they remember the commands they've been taught throughout their life.

memory

Association is central to how a dog learns and it's their associative memory that's doing most of the work as you train them. When a dog remembers by associating, they're linking something specific with what they've seen/tasted/ heard or touched and whether it has a positive or a negative memory. Hence why, when training your dog, creating positive associations is so important in making them want to follow your orders.

Associative memory also provides your dog with secure routine in their lives. Dogs like to know what to expect! Your dog learns incredibly subtle associations that tell them exactly what's coming next. For example, the sound of you opening a cupboard at a certain time of day will set off the sequence of associations in their memory that says, "I'm going to be fed!" Your dog may appear to be dozy and disinterested at times, but they're keeping a close eye on everything you do and storing this information for use at a later date.

Does my dog have a super memory?

Of course, every dog is an individual but these two easy tests will tell you if your dog has a super sharp memory.

Test 1: Short-term memory

With the help of someone else, gently hold your dog in the middle of the room. Show your dog a treat (something they find delicious), let them sniff it and then put the treat in the corner of the room. Take the dog out of the room then, almost immediately, let them back in. If your dog has very poor short-term memory they won't even bother looking for the treat. But if they have an excellent short-term memory, they'll go straight to the hiding place.

Test 2: Long-term memory

This is a variant of Test 1 and you should do it straight afterward. Follow the same steps, but this time remove your dog from the room for five minutes. What do they do when they're back in the room? Again, the quicker they find the treat, the better their long-term memory. You can try extending the time they're out of the room to challenge them (but don't put the treat in the same place each time).

PAWS FOR THOUGHT

Studies have shown that a dog's memory is not based solely on repetition and reward. They have an episodic-like memory, very much like humans do. This means they can recall their own life events – so, yes, they probably do remember that amazing barbecue where they ate your hot dog!

Now you see it...

...Now you don't. But does that mean it no longer exists? Not if it's just hidden. If a tree falls in a forest and no one is around to hear it, does it make a sound? Ask your dog. On second thoughts, let's not get too deeply into the philosophy of observation and perception! All you need to know is that object permanence is a great measure of your dog's cognitive abilities.

Hidden or gone?

'Object permanence' is also used with young children to test their cognitive skills and development. It's all about the ability to recognize that an object doesn't simply vanish or stop existing if you can't see it. Remember that your dog has the cognitive abilities of a two-year-old, so, as always, don't expect too much of them! If you find they're surpassing what the local preschool kids can do, watch out – your dog may be plotting to take over the world!

Take the test

It's very easy to test your dog's understanding of object permanence. You can scale up the levels of difficulty to see how advanced your dog's understanding of the concept is. (Don't make it too hard to start with though as that will just end in frustration for both of you.)

Whilst your dog is watching you, put one of their favorite toys underneath an opaque container or hide it behind a cushion. Don't speak to your dog or encourage them in any way – just watch how they react. If your dog attempts to move the container/cushion to get to their toy, it shows they have a good basic level of understanding of object permanence. Not all dogs have this, so don't be surprised it they don't get it. If they do, shower them with praise – they're one clever hound!

PAWS FOR THOUGHT

Try your VERY hardest not to get involved! Bite your tongue and tie your hands behind your back if you have to! Studies have shown that human interference lowers your dog's ability to understand object permanence. They'll figure it out far better by themselves than with your help.

Brain games:
the classics

There are some things that people just expect every dog to be able to do. And if you're touting your dog about as a genius, you certainly should make sure they can do some of these classic tricks just in case they're asked to perform!

Play dead

Aim of the game: Teaches your dog to lie as still as a corpse. Weirdly cute despite how morbid it is.

Step 1: Get your dog in a lying down position. Using one of their favorite treats, persuade them to turn their head to one side. As they do this, roll them onto their side. (You'll need to practice this step a few times.)

Step 2: Show your dog that the longer they lie in that position, the more treats they'll get! You'll find that this gradually increases the length of time they will stay lying on their side.

Step 3: When your dog is ready, gradually replace the treat with a hand signal that indicates to your dog that it should roll onto its side.

There's a lot for your dog to master in this trick. They need to understand, for example, why you're rolling them onto one side and the benefits of staying there. In their heads, they're not 'playing dead', they're just doing something weird and inexplicable that their owner wants them to do! All your dog knows is that it gets LOTS of praise for doing it. What you know – and they don't – is that it's brilliant stimulation for their brain.

Spin like a tornado

Aim of the game: Teach your dog to spin around in a circle. This is a simple but effective trick to wow the crowds.

Step 1: Hold a treat above your dog's nose and move it in a large circle above its head. They should follow your

hand with their head, but keep trying if it doesn't happen straightaway. When they do follow your hand in a full circle, it's time for lots of praise and treats!

Step 2: When you've both mastered Step 1, start to use the word 'spin' as a cue for your dog to move it's head in a circle. Using its amazing powers of association, your dog will soon learn what you're expecting it to do.

Step 3: To make this even more impressive, you can build up the number of spins your dog does before they're rewarded with a treat. Don't expect too many spins though – they'll just get bored or dizzy!

Step 4: As with all tricks, once your dog understands your verbal prompt, you can stop giving them treats.

Spinning like a tornado is great fun to watch and your dog will enjoy the applause it gets. But it's also very challenging as it relies on them focusing and flexing their ability to learn through association. Work at your dog's pace and be patient – you'll soon have them generating enough wind to power a large city.

Dogs got personality.
Personality goes a long way.

QUENTIN TARANTINO

Dogs are not our whole life,
but they make our
lives whole.

**ROGER CARAS
(PHOTOGRAPHER AND WRITER)**

Unlock your dog's potential

Keeping your dog
stimulated

It's crucial that you keep your dog's brain stimulated, both for their emotional and mental health and their physical health. Throughout their lives, dogs need to be kept active and interested in their surroundings, and this can be challenging for owners. Do you need more toys? Do they need more company? Don't panic. It's not too difficult to find the right balance and the rewards are well worth the effort.

My dog is fine!

Really? Are you sure? Even if you own the most chilled out dog in the world, they still need to have their brain exercised. The same applies if your dog is the bounciest hound in town. Don't be complacent – keeping their brain active is still important. If you think your dog is already a genius, this is all the more reason why you need to work to stop them getting bored (although it's unlikely they'll ever get fed up with playing with a ball). At the other end of the spectrum, if your dog's attitude to life is more sedate, it's time to try and unlock their potential.

How to challenge your dog's mind

Keeping your dog 's grey cells stimulated doesn't need to be taxing. Try doing some of the following activities with them:

- Teach them a new trick. (See Tricky tricks on page 95.)

- Interactive games. If you've visited your pet store recently, you'll have seen shelves full of games for your pet. Canine puzzles, board games, treat catapults – you name it, someone has probably created a doggy version.

- Get them out and about. And not just on a walk around the block! Take them out and about with you while you're running errands. Their brain will be entertained by the new people, sounds, sights and smells they encounter. Anything that makes their senses run wild is brilliant for their brain so let them sniff around and explore.

- Rotate their toys. Yes, parents are advised to do this with their children! But why should your dog's habits be any different? Regularly swap your dog's toys around so that they don't get bored playing with the same ones all the time.

- Brain games. Luckily for you, we've made this easy – try out some of the fun and engaging brain games for your dog that are scattered throughout this book!

The benefits

Keeping your dog's brain stimulated has valuable benefits for you and your dog. It's not rocket science and there are only bonuses to be gained – so what's stopping you?!

The benefits for your dog:

- Banishes boredom. Boredom and negative energy in dogs can lead to all kinds of undesirable behavior, such as chewing furniture and generally being a nuisance.

- Increases their inquisitiveness.

- An alert brain will allow them to adapt better to new situations – and therefore behave better in them!

- Boosts their ability to learn.

- Their lives will be enriched and their happiness levels will soar.

The benefits for you:

- The more you interact with, and pay attention to your dog, the better you'll get at reading their behavior and understanding their body language. And...

- ...the better you'll become at communicating with them effectively to get the outcome you want.

- A happier, less stressed dog is far easier to control. The result: you'll be happier and less stressed too!

Doggy depression

Just like humans, dogs can become depressed. It's fairly easy to tell if your dog is depressed as they'll look incredibly sad. Other signs to look out for include: loss of appetite, changes in behavior and mood, excessive sleeping, hiding, and paw licking. Dogs can experience depression for many reasons, but one of them is a lack of mental and physical stimulation. It doesn't mean that you're a bad owner, but – once you've ruled out any medical factors – you need to explore new and inventive ways to stimulate your dog. And, of course, increase their hug time.

Canine
wordsmiths

Have you ever tried to count how many words your dog understands? Probably not, but if you did you might be surprised. Dogs learn a lot by observing and making associations so if they've regularly heard you say the name of an object when you're using or handling it, they may recognize it. Is there any benefit to teaching your dog a range of words? And if they can remember more than the average dog, does that make them a genius?

The benchmarks

Dogs can learn around 165 words with basic training Some, with more specialist and intense training, can learn up to 250 words. On page 118, you can find out more about Chaser the Collie, who mastered the names of over 1,000 different items. Chaser was certainly extraordinary but it's good to have something to aim for!

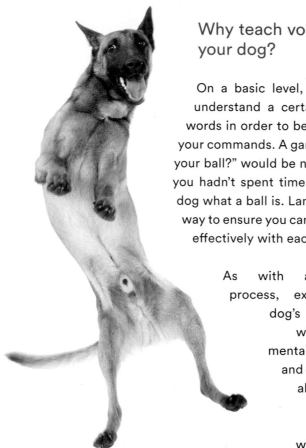

Why teach vocabulary to your dog?

On a basic level, dogs need to understand a certain number of words in order to be able to follow your commands. A game of "Where's your ball?" would be no fun to play if you hadn't spent time teaching your dog what a ball is. Language is a key way to ensure you can communicate effectively with each other.

As with any learning process, extending your dog's understanding will keep them mentally stimulated and challenged. It's also a great way to and build a special bond with your pet.

Getting started

Don't even attempt to teach your dog an abstract concept! Even if your dog is a genius, it's highly unlikely they'll ever understand existentialism. Dogs need to make an association between an object and a spoken word for the idea to lock into their brain. The best way to teach new vocabulary is therefore with repetition and by being – every dog trainer's favorite word – consistent. And remember: ONE WORD, ONE MEANING.

1. Show your dog the object. Use a short, simple sound to immediately connect the sound to the object. For example, if you have a TV remote in your hand, simply call it a 'remote'. Your dog really isn't bothered how accurate you are!

2. Spend some time with your dog playing with the object, making sure there are no other objects around to distract them. Keep using the object's name so that your dog gets used to it.

3. You'll need to be patient as A LOT of repetition is key! You'll get to a point where you can try placing the object somewhere and asking your dog to fetch it. If they do, your patience is paying off. Good job!

4. The next step is to place the object with other household items so that your dog has a selection to pick from. If they select the correct object, they're clearly very clever indeed.

Positive reinforcement plays an important part in teaching your dog something new. Be super-enthusiastic with praise and hugs and modify the tone of your voice – if you keep it light and friendly, your dog will be far more receptive to your training.

PAWS FOR THOUGHT

It can take 50 to 100 repetitions of a word – spoken while your dog performs an action – for the dog to make the connection between the two.

Tricky
tricks

Teaching your dog tricks is an awesome way
of interacting and having fun with them.
Importantly, it also helps keep their brain alert
and active. The whole process of learning tricks
is also useful if you want to discover if your dog
has genius potential – however hidden that might
seem when you start!

Remember to have fun!

Teaching tricks isn't a competition or a test. In fact, the more fun you make it, the more likely it is your dog will pick it up. A stressed dog is not a receptive dog! Be sensitive to their tolerance levels. When you're trying to teach them a new trick, don't work at it for too long or you'll risk them getting bored.

It's also vital that you don't get frustrated with your dog if they don't understand what you're trying to teach them. Your clever pooch needs your patience, nurturing and gentle encouragement if they're going to open their mind!

Try some of these easy tricks to start, then work your way up to more difficult ones depending on your dog's level of genius. Not all dogs 'get' tricks but with A LOT of treats as an incentive, many will!

The handshake trick

This is a simple trick to get started with and forms the foundation for lots of more advanced tricks.

1. Start by asking your dog to sit. Next, say "Shake hands!" and take their paw in your hand. Give them lots of praise and then let go of their paw. Repeat several times and then repeat daily, gradually building up their understanding of what you're expecting them to do.

2. Try asking your dog to 'shake hands' but this time don't take their paw and see what they do. If they lift their paw, you've cracked it. If they don't, well, as with any canine training, keep trying. Like humans, dogs all learn at different speeds.

The hoop-jumping dog trick

Before starting (and to avoid disappointment), make sure your dog actually fits through the hoop!

1. Set the hoop on the ground in front of your dog and call them through, using a treat as an incentive. If they walk through, give them huge amounts of praise and – of course – the treat.

2. On the next pass, lift the hoop slightly off the ground and say "Jump!". You may still need a treat to tempt your dog through the weird circle thing.

3. Each time they master a hoop jump, try next time to raise it a little higher off the ground. They'll soon associate your command with the trick, at which point you can phase out the edible bribes.

The backwards dog trick

1. Start with your dog facing you. Walk towards them and when they take a step backwards lavish them with praise and a treat.

2. Keep repeating this action until your dog can take a few steps back before they receive a treat to reward their efforts.

3. Eventually, you'll be able to replace the promise of a treat with a verbal command that will prompt them to walk backwards, even if you haven't taken a step towards them.

Mastering these simple tricks provides your dog with some hugely beneficial brain stimulation and sets them up for the challenge of tackling harder tasks. What's more, when you show off their new-found skills to friends, your dog will adore the praise that rains down on them. Happy brain, happy dog!

PAWS FOR THOUGHT

The more you train your dog, the better you'll become at teaching and the better your dog will become at learning. You're quite a team! As with anything, practice makes perfect – for both of you.

Anybody who doesn't know
what soap tastes like never
washed a dog.

FRANKLIN P. JONES

Every dog is
unique

Clever dogs:
the
downsides

There are lots of brilliant benefits to owning a clever dog: they listen and respond to commands and they snuggle up to you when you're feeling down, to name just two. But are there any downsides to owning a highly intelligent pooch? It's important to be aware of the potential problems and challenges if you want to ensure your dog stays healthy and happy.

Did you know?

- Clever dogs often have lots and lots of energy and therefore need extra physical (as well as mental) stimulation.

- Smarter dogs get bored easily and you'll need to work hard to keep them entertained. Like children, this boredom can manifest itself as an inability to pay attention, a lack of interest in additional learning and generally unacceptable behavior.

- To successfully train a clever dog, you need to take account of how quickly their minds move. If you repeat the same training exercises over and over again, they'll soon get fed up. Turn the demands of the training up a notch and ensure you're offering them a variety of new challenges.

- If your dog is clever, it's more likely to pick up bad habits. They learn by observing things so don't assume that they'll only learn what you specifically teach or show them. Who knows the consequences of seeing you sitting on the couch picking your nose...

What do they need from you?

Owning a dog is a two-way relationship. Your dog provides you with companionship, fun and love. You provide your dog with much the same, plus food, exercise and shelter – basically everything they need to be fit and healthy, physically and emotionally. Be warned: if you have a highly intelligent dog, you're going to need to keep up with them – they won't wait for you to catch up!

PAWS FOR THOUGHT

Research with the famously clever Border Collie, Chaser, showed that while she was brilliant at logic and memory games, she lacked empathy and communication skills – two things that pet owners love about their dogs. Brains or love? We know which we'd choose!

Essential resumé skills for owning a genius dog include:

- Inventiveness. You need to be constantly thinking of new ideas for games to play and things to do to prevent your dog from getting bored. You don't want them twiddling their paws.

- Energy. Lots of it! Smart dogs are more energetic so you'll need your own get-up-and-go to ensure your dog gets all the exercise and stimulation it needs. There's no time for slacking when your dog lives life at 1,000 miles per hour!

- Ability to adapt. Know when your dog is bored and it's time to move onto something else. Whilst you might be wanting to perfect heelwork, if it's not challenging your dog then drop your plans and move onto something else. You might find this frustrating but it won't be as annoying as dealing with a bored dog that refuses to listen and learn.

Brain games:
walkies!

These two games are perfect for when you and your dog are out on a walk. Time to think beyond just throwing a stick or a chewed up baseball!

Find me!

Aim of the game: Challenge your dog to use their detective powers to find you. They'll need to use their ears and eyes, plus their knowledge that things that go missing haven't just disappeared!

Step 1: When your dog is distracted, find yourself a good hiding place. Try not to go too far – you want your dog to successfully find you rather than them give up and go home!

Step 2: Call your dog's name – use a tone that encourages and excites them. Keep calling them so that they get the chance to figure out where you are and head to the exact spot. As soon as they find you, give them a whole heap of praise and they'll feel they've achieved something amazing.

The more times you play this game, the more quickly your dog will be able to find you. You'll find yourself having to call them less and less as they become masters of hide and seek.

Obstacle course

Aim of the game: To use the landscape and environment around you as a fun, stimulating obstacle course.

Obstacle course fun doesn't need to be all about seesaws and jumps and tunnels! When you're out for a walk, make use of your surroundings to create your own obstacle race. All you need is a bit of creativity.

For example:

- Weave back and forth between a row of trees.
- Take a detour up and down a flight of stairs.

- Run up a hill and down the other side.

- Leap over logs.

- Jump off small walls, benches, etc.

- Encourage your dog to jump in muddy puddles!

Whilst being a fantastic physical workout that releases energy (for both of you!), this activity will also keep your dog's brain active. They'll need to focus on you for instructions and think quickly for themselves about each new challenge.

If you head out for the same walk in the same direction past the same things at the same time every day, then both you and your dog will inevitably get bored. When you vary your route, you'll encounter more stimuli and lots of new things for your dog to see, hear and, most excitingly for them, smell.

Less intelligent dogs:
the upsides!

Do you really want your dog to be a genius? Everyone wants something different from their pet. There are so many types of 'clever', is it really possible to find a dog that's a genius at everything? If you prefer kooky to geeky then read on...

Your less clever dog is awesome because...

- ...they are less demanding and less fussy.

- ...they tend to be more sociable and better at establishing emotional connections, making them fantastic playmates.

- ...they may take longer to train but they're more likely to follow commands once they've learnt them. Smarter dogs can be quite rebellious and have an urge to break rules.

- ...they can be more tolerant, less likely to pester you and are keen to keep the peace.

Is my dog just under-stimulated?

If your dog doesn't seem to understand or respond to commands (or ever learn that taunting next door's cat always leads to a paw swipe around the head), you might assume they're stupid. However, it could be that they're just under-stimulated and therefore BORED. You, as an owner, are the key to unlocking your dog's full potential. No pressure!

Signs that your dog is under-stimulated include: misbehaving to get attention, not responding to their name being called, barking, chewing, jumping up or pacing the floor. If you spot any of these signs, it's time to consider whether you're sufficiently stimulating your dog.

Consider whether they need longer walks (perhaps in different places with new things to see), more toys, something appropriate to chew (rather than the furniture) or more interaction with you (are they feeling lonely?). See page 80 for some more great ideas on how to keep your dog's brain stimulated.

Dumb but adorable

Who says it's the 'clever' dogs like Lassie and the Littlest Hobo that should be the ones to steal the limelight? Have a look at these fictional dogs that weren't blessed with brains but are still superstars:

Odie: Garfield's kooky canine companion. Odie's idiocy is a running gag throughout the comic strip.

Reddy: Star of *Ruff and Reddy*, an animated series about the adventures of a smart cat and a not-so-smart dog. We're detecting a theme here! Who writes these scripts? Cats?

PAWS FOR THOUGHT

Intelligence doesn't equal happiness.
Enough said!

Goofy: It's all in the name. One of Disney's most famous dogs, Goofy is clumsy and dim-witted, yet – in his own charming way – his hidden intelligence often shines through.

Dug: If any dog proves that intelligence isn't about what you know but what you do, it's Dug in the tearjerking Disney movie, *Up*. Dug has a device on his collar that translates his thoughts into English. "My name is Dug and I have just met you and I love you" reveals what simple beings dogs are. Dug may not be the smartest cookie but he is full of love and utterly loyal.

Scooby-Doo: Adorably goofy and somewhat lacking in the brains department, this super sleuth still manages to solve many of the cases that the Mystery, Inc. team takes on.

Older
dogs

There's so much to learn about how to boost your dog's intelligence from the puppy period through to adulthood. But what happens to your dog's brain as it gets older? Like humans, there comes a point when we must accept the limitations that old age brings. However, this doesn't mean that you should stop trying to stimulate your dog's brain.

Keeping your dog active

As well as keeping your older dog physically active, keeping their brain active is very important. Regardless of their age, they'll still succumb to boredom (and potentially depression) if you don't provide the stimulation they need. They won't have the same boundless energy as a pup, but they'll still respond to positive encouragement. Despite what they say, you can teach an old dog new tricks!

Doggie dementia

Canine Cognitive Dysfunction Syndrome (CCDS) is very similar to Alzheimer's disease in humans. Sadly, it's something that dogs may suffer from as they get older, usually when they're over 11 years old. Your dog might start to show signs of confusion, anxiety, listlessness, wandering, aggression and changes in their normal behavioral and sleeping patterns.

The good news is that by stimulating your dog with games and toys you can help stop the symptoms of CCDS from worsening. Play with them just as you would normally, just be sensitive to the fact you'll need to adapt activities to suit them and their comfort levels. You might find that their patience isn't as good as it used to be, so don't stimulate them to the point of irritation.

A boy can learn a lot from
a dog: obedience, loyalty, and
the importance of
turning around three times
before lying down.

ROBERT BENCHLEY

Dogs are better than human
beings because they know
but do not tell.

EMILY DICKINSON

The lighter side of genius

Top dog geniuses

These dogs are truly worthy of the accolade of 'genius'. Each story pays testimony to dogs' amazing abilities – whether it's their capacity to learn and observe or their wonderful capacity for love. Every one of these dogs is super smart in their own way. Perfect inspirational (and motivational) bedtime stories to read to your own dog!

Chaser the Collie

World-renowned Chaser goes down in doggie records as perhaps the smartest dog of all time. She was trained to understand over 1,000 nouns (even the cleverest dogs struggle to learn more than 250 words) but it didn't come without effort: her owner trained her for four to five hours per day over the course of three years! He would show Chaser an object, say its name around 40 times and then hide it for her to find.

Buddy the German Shepherd

Buddy's owner owes his life to his clever canine. Because he suffered from frequent seizures, he taught Buddy how to dial the emergency services by hitting the speed dial button on the telephone. When Buddy's help was urgently needed, this well-trained dog knew exactly what to do and his quick response saved his owner's life.

Stella the Catahoula and Blue Heeler mix

Stella's owner has been teaching her to use a series of buttons to communicate since Stella was eight weeks old. Each button is labeled with a word, for example 'ball' and 'walk'. By tapping the buttons with her paw, Stella can hear the word and can construct sentences to ask her owner for things or express an emotion or need.

Tillman the English Bulldog

Forget everything this book said earlier about Bulldogs not being the brightest of breeds! Amazing Tillman taught himself to master the art of skateboarding. He's also a Guinness World Record Holder and in 2009 became the world's fastest skateboarding dog, traveling 100m in less than 20 seconds! This adrenaline junkie also enjoys snowboarding and surfing.

Red the Lurcher

Staff at Battersea Dogs and Cats Home in London couldn't figure out why they kept finding dogs on the loose and food missing from the kitchen. To solve the mystery, they installed surveillance cameras. The footage showed clever Red breaking out of his kennel and then letting other dogs out for a midnight feast and party every night!

Orlando the Labrador

All service dogs are absolute heroes. Orlando is a service dog and when his blind owner fainted on a subway platform and fell onto the tracks, Orlando immediately came to his rescue. After trying to tug his owner away from the edge, Orlando leapt down onto the tracks and tried to wake him up by licking and kissing him. Miraculously, both survived a train rolling over the top of them.

Silla the German Shepherd

Silla was stolen from his owner in Turkey before being dumped and attacked by stray dogs. Super-smart Silla managed to find his way to hospital by following ambulances, somehow making the connection between those vehicles and receiving help. Thankfully, Silla made a speedy recovery after being treated by a doctor at the hospital. Clever and resourceful – Silla is one amazing dog.

Barry the Saint Bernard

Saint Bernards are well-known for their huge size and amazing mountain rescue skills. Barry became famous in the early 1800s for saving 40 lives. His most famous rescue was of a small child who had become trapped on a dangerous ice shelf. Barry reached the boy and kept him warm until rescue came. However, the rescue team were unable to reach the pair so the boy climbed onto Barry's back and was slowly dragged to safety.

Just for
fun

Keeping your clever dog's brain stimulated is hard work. Time to take a break and enjoy something a bit more light hearted...

What do chemists' dogs do with their bones?

They barium!

What is a dog's favorite type of homework to do?

A lab report.

Why shouldn't dogs work the TV remote?

They always hit the paws button!

How are a dog and a marine biologist alike?

One wags a tail and the other tags a whale!

What do you do if a dog chews your dictionary?

Take the words right out of its mouth!

What does a dog get when it finishes obedience school?

Their pet-degree!

I went to the zoo – all they had was one small dog.

It was a shih-tzu.

What happens when you buy a dog from a blacksmith?

As soon as it gets home, it makes a bolt for the door.

What's more amazing than a talking dog?

A spelling bee.

What do you get when you cross a dog and an abacus?

A friend you can count on.

What did the dog get when it multiplied 123 by 466?

The wrong answer, it's a dog.

I threw a ball for my dog last night.

Well, he does look great in a tux.

Why can't humans hear a dog whistle?

Because dogs can't whistle.

My dog kept chasing people on a bike.

Eventually, it got so bad I had to take his bike away.

A woman walked by a table in a hotel and noticed three men and a dog playing cards.

"That is a very smart dog." the woman commented.

"He's not so smart," said one of the players.

"Every time he gets a good hand he wags his tail."

After a talking sheepdog gets
all the sheep in the pen, he
reports back to the farmer:
"All 40 accounted for."
"But I only have 36 sheep,"
says the farmer.
"I know," says the sheepdog.
"But I rounded them up."

Test your knowledge!

So, you think your dog is clever. But how about you? Have we kept your brain cells active? Time to test whether you've been paying attention as much as your dog has. We can't incentivize you with a treat, but we've helped by making the test multiple choice. Answers at the end of the quiz!

1. **Your dog has the same cognitive skills as a:**

    (a) 2-year-old child

    (b) 3-year-old child

    (c) 4-year-old child

2. **How many smell receptors does a dog have in its nose?**

    (a) 150 million

    (b) 250 million

    (c) 50 million

3. **Which is the brainiest breed of dog?**

    (a) Border Collie

    (b) Rottweiler

    (c) Golden Retriever

4. **How many degrees of peripheral vision does a dog have?**

    (a) 180 degrees

    (b) 250 degrees

    (c) 300 degrees

5. How many muscles does a dog have in each ear?

   (a) 10

   (b) 18

   (c) 20

6. Which of these is a sign that your dog might be confused?

   (a) Lies down on the floor and completely ignores you

   (b) Eats more food

   (c) Starts digging up the garden

7. What was Albert Einstein's dog called?

   (a) Chico Marx

   (b) Groucho Marx

   (c) Karl Marx

8. How many words can a dog learn with basic training?

   (a) 100

   (b) 165

   (c) 190

9. How many repetitions of a word can it take before your dog connects it to an action?

   (a) 10 to 50

   (b) 50 to 100

   (c) 100 to 150

10. Tillman the English Bulldog broke a world speed record using which mode of travel?

    (a) Roller-skates

    (b) Snowboard

    (c) Skateboard

Answers

1. (a), 2. (b), 3. (a), 4. (b), 5. (b), 6. (a), 7. (a), 8. (b), 9. (b), 10. (c).

Genius
training notes

Use the space below to record of any observations you've made about your dog's super brain power! Most of all, have fun!